First published in Great Britain 2024 by Red Shed, part of Farshore
An imprint of HarperCollins*Publishers*
1 London Bridge Street,
London SE1 9GF
www.farshore.co.uk

HarperCollins*Publishers*
Macken House, 39/40 Mayor Street Upper
Dublin 1, D01 C9W8

Text © HarperCollins*Publishers* Limited 2024.
Written by Hannah Wilson.
Illustrations © Peter Phobia 2024.
Peter Phobia has asserted his moral rights.
Consultancy by Neil Ellis.

ISBN 978 0 00 861410 2
Printed in Malaysia.
001

A CIP catalogue record for this title is available from the British Library.

Stay safe online. Any website addresses listed in this book are correct
at the time of going to print. However, Farshore is not responsible for content
hosted by third parties. Please be aware that online content can be subject
to change and websites can contain content that is unsuitable for children.
We advise that all children are supervised when using the internet.

Always ask an adult for help with any craft activity or DIY project. Wear
protective clothes and cover surfaces to avoid damage or staining.

This book contains FSC™ certified paper and other controlled
sources to ensure responsible forest management.

For more information visit: www.harpercollins.co.uk/green

CONTENTS

SUPER-IMPORTANT SAFETY STUFF!

OK, let's face facts: skateboarding involves a risk of injury. So get thinking about how to reduce that risk. Grab a parent or guardian and check out your national skateboard organization's website. Are there top tips about how to learn safely?

Pad up! Always wear a snugly fitted helmet, knee and elbow pads and wrist guards. Flat-soled trainers provide better grip (and look good too, right?).

Investigate the skatespot – are the obstacles and surfaces safe for you and your skills? Never skate on or near roads or vehicles! And look around you – give plenty of space to other skaters and non-skaters. Finally, go skating with a parent, guardian or instructor.

READY TO ROLL

Just a small board on four wheels. Awesome fun, right? But did you know that the simple skateboard has, for more than 70 years, blazed a trail through culture, fashion, sport and our urban landscapes? What does that even mean?! I hear you asking. Well, we're going to find out and help you on your own skateboarding journey along the way.

You're part of a worldwide community, but it's up to you how you roll. So have a think about what you like about skateboarding: Perhaps you're happy just goofing around with mates? It doesn't matter what you can or can't do as long as you're safe and having fun.

> "SKATEBOARDING HAS ALWAYS BEEN ABOUT FREEDOM AND CREATIVITY AND BEING DIFFERENT."
>
> *Danny Way, aerial master*
> Speaking in 2005 film I Am Danny Way

But if you do want to improve your technique, start small, low and slow. Build up a foundation of basic skills before trying harder stuff. But how? Think about different ways to learn. Can you practise with friends, have lessons with an instructor or watch online tutorials with your parent or guardian? Chat with them about risk. What are the potential dangers and are you comfortable with them?

8

Can you make them smaller? Yes, we're talking helmets, pads and practice – but anything else?

It's great to be inspired by the pros, but comparing yourself to them and others is not always helpful – their tricks may not be right for you just yet. What tricks can you practise at your current skill level?

Once you've thought about all this, you'll be good to go. Hit the skatepark and push yourself towards great things. Go for it!

So, ready to roll? Let's rustle up some deck designs, drop in on the sickest skatespots, meet the legends, change the world (well, we can try) and even power down some mighty megaramps at mighty megacomps.

Oh, and if you find a skate term that you're unfamiliar with, check out the glossary on pages 44–45.

GRAB YOUR BOARD: LET'S GO . . . .

EXPRESS YOURSELF

You might live in a pair of scuffed up skate shoes and seek out eye-popping graffiti to cruise past or, well, you might not. The way you express your love for skating is totally down to who you are. Skateboarding can be a way of life that influences fashion, art and music, and many who love to roll leave behind a trail of decorated decks, cool clothes and arty videos. So what's *your* vibe?

DO A...

KICKFLIP

YOUR VIBE ATTRACTS YOUR TRIBE
Bring your own thing to the ramp and you could well find your tribe. Perhaps a kids' crew – like Subsect from Des Moines, USA, who dress up at Halloween to shred the local skatepark. Or would a skate-punk tribe be more your vibe? Or how about the Bolivian crew from La Paz who skate in skirts and tall hats?

SOLO STYLE

You don't need a crew to be you. You might prefer to skate solo. Just remember to skate for fun, whatever fun means for you – whether that's gliding through parks, riding ramps or practising tricks.

"What skateboarding has given me is a form of expression to express and be who I wanted to be . . ."

Rodney Mullen, freestyle legend
Speaking in 2012 at the Smithsonian museum's Lemelson Center in Washington DC, USA, about how skateboarding and invention overlap

SHAPE UP

Which shape works for you? A thrashin' fishtail or a classic popsicle? Wider decks are more stable, and your shoe size will affect how wide the board feels.

Popsicle boards are also known as twin-tips.

STICK IT

For flips that really pop, decorate the underside of your deck with stickers!

That's one cool customizer.

BLING BLING!

In 2014, the world's most expensive skateboard went on sale with a price tag of £9,000 – the board was plated in super-shiny GOLD!

GET ON BOARD

Good news: unlike the early 1950s, you no longer have to fasten roller-skate wheels to a plank of wood. Phew! Today, you can choose a ready-made board in a shape, size and colour that suits your style. Or, with a grown-up, you can get creative and customize your set up. Then you do you!

HOW TO PAINT YOUR DECK'S UNDERSIDE:

1. Take off the trucks.
2. Use sandpaper to remove old paint.
3. Tape over parts you don't want to repaint.
4. Go crazy with colourful acrylic paint!
5. When dry, remove tape and coat with clear varnish.

GET A GRIP

Forget the grey sandpaper look – paint your griptape, perhaps using a homemade stencil. If your deck is blank, paint or sticker it, then seal over with clear griptape to protect your work. Or find colourful, patterned tape and cut it into a jagged jigsaw design.

FEEL THE WHEELS

Thank your lucky stars that wheels are no longer made of bone-rattling metal! From the early 1970s, they've been polyurethane, a type of rubbery plastic. Choose small, harder wheels for street tricks or large, softer ones for ripping up ramps. Find colourful wheels (and bearings) or dye them yourself – try to use a planet-friendly eco dye.

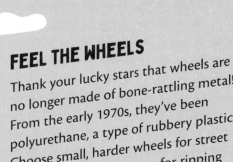

TINKER WITH TRUCKS

These T-shaped bits of metal need to be rail-grindingly tough, but they don't have to be boring. Unbolt them and spray paint them. If you can, use coloured nuts and bolts when you reattach the trucks.

Use a ruler to smooth down stickers and avoid wrinkles!

DECK-ORATE

When you're not shredding the skatepark, hang your board on your bedroom wall (check with an adult first). An old deck, painted or polished, makes a great bookshelf!

BUS-SIZED BOARD!

The largest skateboard ever built was 11.14m long – the size of a bus. Once, it rolled down a hill and was about to crash, so the rider had to jump off. It was way too big and heavy to steer!

Spray paint outdoors with an adult!

Fear dribbles? Try a paint pen.

70s SURF SKATE

When surfers moved from beach to skateboard in the 1970s, they took their short shorts and tight T-shirts with them. And as if they were surfing, they often went barefoot. (Scratchy griptape wasn't common until the mid-70s.) When shoes were worn, socks were often white, knee-high and striped.

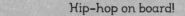

HEAD TO TOE

Over the years, skaters have expressed themselves through their clothes and shoes. They weren't afraid to be different, but they were influenced by the culture around them, whether it was 80s punk or 90s hip-hop. Today, skateboarding influences everyday, high-street fashion, and millions of skate shoes are sold to people who don't ride.

80s SKATE-PUNK

In the 1980s, punk, grunge and rock music were added to the skate mix of colourful pads and high socks. Rock-band T-shirts, bandanas, ripped denim and serious attitude mixed up skating and pulled it in all directions, away from its surfing roots.

Who doesn't like a hoodie?

In 1976, Z-Boys Tony Alva and Stacy Peralta (see pages 18–19) designed the first shoe for skateboarding.

High-top basketball shoes offered good ankle support as skateboarders went vert in the 1980s.

BIG IN THE 90s

As hip-hop music brought many skate videos to life in the 1990s, rap kids and skate kids connected, and their clothing styles merged too. Oversized T-shirts and baggy jeans became the uniform of many skaters. The loose clothing allowed more movement as technical street skating developed – and the tough denim protected skaters from serious sidewalk slams.

Street skaters in the 1990s needed more ankle flexibility. They cut the tops off Steve Caballero's pro shoe, inspiring Vans to create the iconic Half Cab.

2000s TO NOW

From the 2000s, jeans got skinny, then wide again, trouser length went up and down, and T-shirts fought with checked shirts for attention. Multi-pocketed cargo trousers and hoodies have long been popular. But remember – they're only clothes. Wear whatever feels comfortable for *you*.

PAD UP!

You know what's less cool than wearing a helmet and pads? A broken bone or a bump on your head, that's what! We recommend that all children pop on pads and a helmet before skating.

By the early 2000s, skate shoes had puffed up. Some loved the chunky, wide shoes; others called them 'cyberpunk baked potatoes'.

GET ON FILM

Ever tried to explain why you love skating to someone who can't tell a skateboard from a scooter? Hard work, right? But show them a photo or video and the magic of skating is there for all to see. So let's get creative and get on film!

VIDEO VISION

To capture the energy of jumps, the graceful lines of runs, the screeching of wheels, nothing can beat video. In the 1980s, home video cameras were big, heavy and pricey. But tech in the 90s delivered cameras small enough to be held in one hand, with motion sensors to avoid shaky shots. Today, smartphones, tiny helmet-mounted cameras and drones can make any skater look pro.

The fish-eye lens of the VX1000 camcorder, introduced in 1995, curved skate action into one shot.

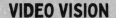

THE POWER OF PRINT

Before the internet, skateboarders shared news in magazines. The first-ever skate mag was *The Quarterly Skateboarder*, printed in the US in 1964 – it cost 50 cents, which is about £4 in today's money. With a grown-up, check out modern skate magazines at your local skate shop or online.
Can you share your skate news by submitting a photo or some writing to a magazine or school newsletter?

ART IN MOTION

Art and skating often go hand-in-hand, with many skaters expressing love for their board through creative projects. Street legend Mark Gonzales (see page 28) was so inspired by the equal upturns of noses and tails that he joined nine skateboards together and skated his art, 'Circle Board', along the streets of New York!

Stay safe online. Websites can be weird, so always get an adult's thumbs-up before searching for anything. And never post your personal info. OK, lecture over!

ON BOARD, ONLINE

Pros often post videos online. Before you watch them, grab a grown-up and your common sense. You probably already know that some stuff is just for pros. Don't feel bad if you can't do it. Work out what's right for *you*. And work out when it's time to put down that device, go outside and get skating!

Experiment with different colour filters for your photos – or choose black and white for a retro look.

PERFECT PICTURES

A picture can say a thousand words, so let snaps of your skating do the talking. Take test shots from different angles to see what works best. Crouching low will add drama and give ollies extra height. Do you want to focus on feet and board, or go for a wide shot that includes the surroundings and tells a different story? Try both!

THE WORLD IS A SKATEPARK

When the long, hot summer of 1976 sucked swimming pools dry (yup – they literally all dried up!), young Californian surfers grabbed their skateboards and dived in anyway. As they soared into the air above the steep sides of the pools, skateboarding was changed forever – pool-like bowls were scooped out of skateparks and vert ramps aimed sky-high.

THE Z-BOYS OF DOGTOWN

When Zephyr surf shop in 'Dogtown' – a rundown coastal area of Los Angeles, USA – started handing out blue team T-shirts to 12 local surfers, the Z-Boys were born. It was 1975 and the 12 young skateboarders, who included Tony Alva, Stacy Peralta and Peggy Oki (the only woman), took competitions by storm. It was all about style, crouching low, hands sweeping the ground, as if riding waves rather than cement.

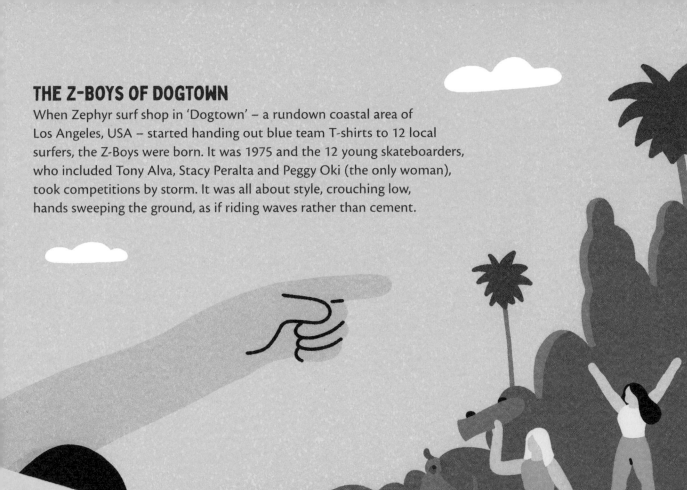

THE RISE OF THE POOL-RIDERS

For Tony Alva and the Z-Boys, empty swimming pools were the perfect playground. It's hard to know exactly who was the first pool-rider to fly up above the edge, turn and drop back down. But Tony's 1977 frontside air was a huge moment, and when a picture of it appeared in *SkateBoarder* magazine, everyone wanted a bit of the action. For Tony, the world was a skatepark and it was this vision – plus his supersick airs – that launched transition skateboarding.

"Skateboarding takes you to the next level, where you really don't need a wave . . . All you need is your board."

Tony Alva, skateboard pioneer, surfer, Z-Boy
Interview with Henry Kingsford for Greyskatemag in 2016

PARK LIFE

Trundling along thin wooden tracks on stilts was pretty much the best the mid-1960s could offer for the first-ever skateparks. Today, huge modern parks have curves, ramps and truck-trashing obstacles. South Korean artist Koo Jeong A has created glow-in-the-dark bowls, and a giant skateable snake lies in an art park in Florida, USA! What would your dream skatepark look like? Let's get planning!

MAKE SPACE

Do you want a massive flow park or a mini street plaza? Will it be outdoors for fun in the sun or indoors for rainy days? How many skaters could it fit? Get the size right and add more floors for more space. The world's first purpose-built, multi-storey skatepark – F51 in Kent, UK – has 2,100m^2 of skating over three levels: one each for bowl, street and flow.

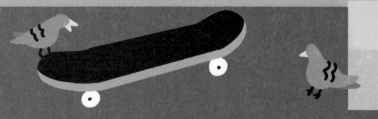

Will your skatepark blend into public areas or be fenced off? For safety, make it clear if stairs are for skaters or pedestrians!

BRANCHING OUT

The locals in La Paz, Bolivia, went all out to create their dream park. Trees and boulders sit among the banks and bowls, old branches are used for coping, and one entrance is a long, curving slide!

THINK GREEN

Plant planet-friendly trees and grass for soft landings. To cut down on car journeys, make your park accessible by board and bike. Is there room for bike racks? Recycling bins and a fountain to fill up water bottles will keep your park clean and green.

FANTASY FEATURES

Don't forget awesome features with flowing lines to link them together. Include classics – there's a reason why every park needs a ramp and a rail. But take inspiration from the world too. Volcanoes and pyramids have already been skate-ified, and the Z-Boys gifted us pool-like bowls. What could *you* invent? Sketch out some ideas.

MATERIAL MATTERS

Skateboards love concrete, but it takes huge amounts of water, energy and raw materials to make it. Plywood may need to be replaced more often, so check out new, greener concretes being developed. And try to reuse old materials. One US company makes ramps out of mushrooms! The fungi bond with rice and corn husks to make super-solid building blocks!

Bright, contrasting colours guide skaters with limited vision. Bumpy 'rumble strips' help them feel their way around.

WHAT CAN YOU DO?

Skatepark etiquette creates a safer, more friendly space for all.

- Be patient and wait your turn. No snaking!
- Stand back from the edge while waiting and drop in only when the ramp or bowl is clear.
- Be aware of others. Give them space to skate freely.
- Don't skate across the bottom of ramps.
- Don't sit or dump your stuff on skateable areas.

ALL TERRAIN

Skateboarders see the world differently. Every smooth slope, ramp or rail could offer an exciting new ride, and potential 'skateparks' pop up in unexpected places – underground, in the desert, high in the air, and even in places designed for water rather than skaters to flow.

PIPE DREAMS

Huge concrete pipes, abandoned in deserts or tunnelling under city streets, have tempted skaters since the early 1970s. With no flat bottoms, the circles propel riders backwards and forwards, pushing them up into bold over-verticals. Only about 20 skateboarders have ever managed full-loops, often on smaller purpose-built pipes with crash pads nearby.

ROCK AND ROLL

Think only bikes can ride real rock? Think again. Sand dunes in the deserts of Utah, USA, turned to stone millions of years ago, forming a natural skatepark with quarter-pipes, ledges and rocky runs!

If rock is mountain-bikeable, it may be skateable too.

Concrete pipes can be 8m high – taller than a two-storey house!

SKATEPARK IN THE SKY!

SKATEPARK IN THE SKY!

A group of filmmakers once skateboarded on a helipad, 212m up one of the world's tallest hotels – Burj Al Arab in Dubai, United Arab Emirates. Gulp!

Is this a slash grind or a splash grind?

MAKING A SPLASH

Only a skateboarder would wish that a water park had no water. Imagine snaking down those tube slides! That dream came true in 2019 for Tony Hawk (see page 30) and his friends. They carved up an abandoned water park in Palm Springs, USA. Tony even full-looped on a giant tube designed for rafts, not wheels!

WHAT CAN YOU DO?

These adventures are for pros with support teams. But take a look around and – with a parent or guardian – work out which spots are skateable for *you*. Ask yourself:

- Am I allowed to skate there?
- How could I skate in a way that is respectful and safe for me, the surroundings and any passers-by?
- Could a skatepark be the best spot for me?
- How can I have new adventures there?

DIY DREAMS

No skatepark near you? No problem! Skaters have been working with what they've got for years, building half-pipes in gardens, transforming abandoned urban spaces and dreaming big with giant homemade megaramps. If you want something doing, do it yourself!

ANSELMO'S HOUSE

Imagine throwing away all the furniture in your home, knocking down walls and making every surface skateable – complete with ramps for jumping through windows! Sounds crazy, right? Well, it's exactly what Anselmo Arruda did to his house in Brazil. He calls it 'Cave House' – because bats live there too!

SALT GRINDER

High up in the Andes Mountains in Bolivia, there is a desert of salt, not sand. It's rough, crumbly, boiling hot during the day and freezing cold at night. And it's blown about by fierce windstorms too! Not the ideal place for skateboarders, right? Wrong. In 2018, a crew of pros helped carve a salty skatepark!

You may want a megaramp in the living room, but – newsflash – your parents or guardians may not! Check with them before you delve into DIY.

BOB GOES BIG

Everything US-Brazilian pro Bob Burnquist does is super-sized. Not only has he racked up a record-breaking haul of 30 medals at the X Games, with eight golds for Big Air, he also owns the world's largest permanent ramp at 'Dreamland', his private skatepark near San Diego, USA. This DIY megaramp monster is 110m long, and speeds of up to 88km/h can launch Bob over its massive 21m gap. He even jumped from a helicopter to ride the ramp. Wheeee!

BUILDING BURNSIDE

Under a bridge in Portland, Oregon, USA, there was once an old, dingy carpark. In the summer of 1990, local skaters slapped concrete against a wall to make a transition, and the world's first DIY skatepark was born. Over the years, quarter-pipes, bowls, pyramids and rails were added. Today, Burnside skatepark is a safe place where local skaters keep building and keep rolling.

WHAT CAN YOU DO?

Got a DIY skate dream? Make it come true by grabbing a grown-up to help, then:

- Sketch out some ideas.
- Research how to make a portable ramp or block to grind.
- Note down materials, tools and building instructions.
- Talk to your teachers – can you use the playground for a skateboard club?

RAMP RAFT

Who knew that skateboarders and snorkellers would make the perfect team? Bob Burnquist did in 2014! Every time he pinged his board off his floating wooden ramp on Lake Tahoe, USA, a snorkeller swam down to rescue it!

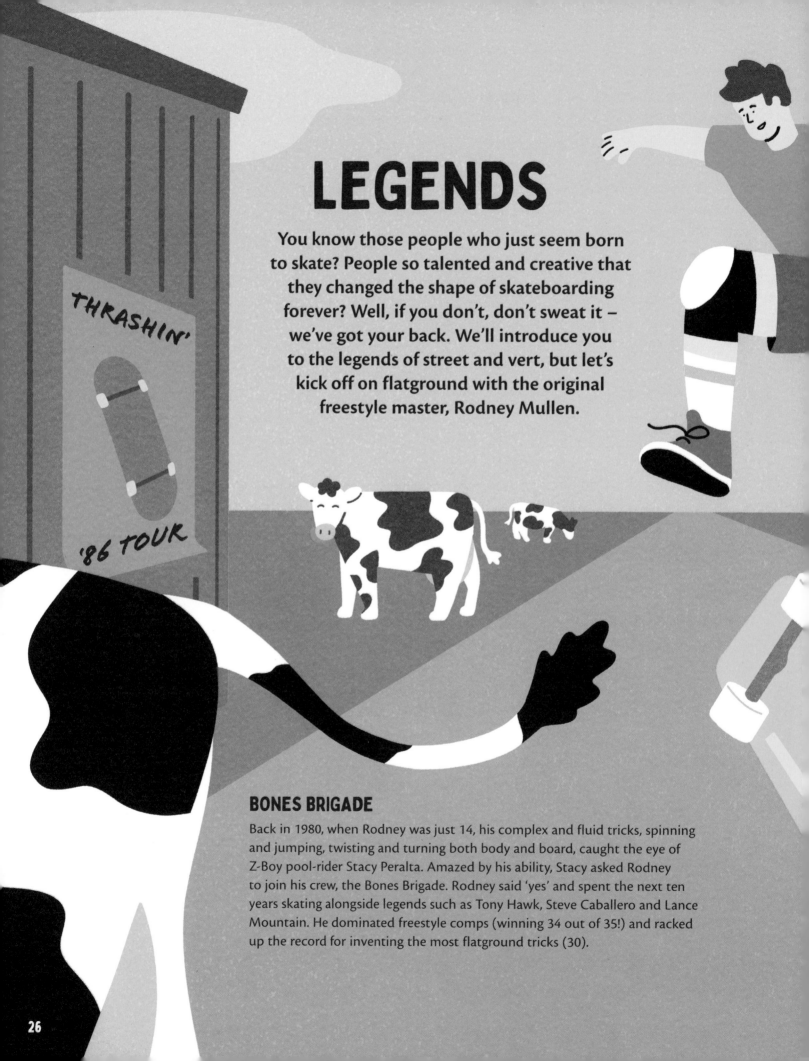

LEGENDS

You know those people who just seem born to skate? People so talented and creative that they changed the shape of skateboarding forever? Well, if you don't, don't sweat it – we've got your back. We'll introduce you to the legends of street and vert, but let's kick off on flatground with the original freestyle master, Rodney Mullen.

THRASHIN'

'86 TOUR

BONES BRIGADE

Back in 1980, when Rodney was just 14, his complex and fluid tricks, spinning and jumping, twisting and turning both body and board, caught the eye of Z-Boy pool-rider Stacy Peralta. Amazed by his ability, Stacy asked Rodney to join his crew, the Bones Brigade. Rodney said 'yes' and spent the next ten years skating alongside legends such as Tony Hawk, Steve Caballero and Lance Mountain. He dominated freestyle comps (winning 34 out of 35!) and racked up the record for inventing the most flatground tricks (30).

THE MAGIC FLIP

Skateboarding history was made on a garage driveway on a farm in Florida, USA. It was the early 1980s and a teenaged Rodney, padded up to keep a promise to his father, was trying to ollie higher and higher. He accidentally flipped the board with his foot, and it spun around and landed perfectly on its wheels, with Rodney next to it. Soon, Rodney was able to land on the board too, and the modern kickflip was born. His friends, baffled, called it the 'magic flip'.

"The biggest obstacle to creativity is breaking through the barrier of disbelief."

Rodney Mullen, freestyle fanatic
*Speaking about perseverance in 2013
TEDx Talk On Getting Up Again,
Costa Mesa, California, USA*

STREET STARS

It wasn't until Rodney Mullen's ollie launched skaters onto steps, rails and benches that city architecture was suddenly seen as the perfect playground and street skating exploded. Boom!

THE GONZ

Back in the mid-80s, on a short handrail in Westwood, California, USA, Mark Gonzales and his pal Natas Kaupas landed the first boardslides. The streets were Mark's playground and he was their master, smashing out unthinkable grinds, ollieing giant gaps and mixing things up with switch-stance skating.

SUPERSICK STEAMER

When someone at the local bike shop lent Elissa Steamer a skateboard in the 1980s, she jumped from BMX to board. She rode all the way to four golds for Street at the X Games in the 2000s. But it was the 90s that had made her a superstar, when videos of her effortlessly gnarly tricks and eye-watering slams took the skateboarding world by storm, and – bam! – in 1998, she became the first female street pro.

In 1999, Elissa became a playable character in the *Tony Hawk's Pro Skater* video game.

FLIGHT CLUB!

With five X Games gold medals for Street, Brazilian Leticia Bufoni is a comp legend. In 2022, she aimed even higher, grinding a rail out of a plane, 2,750m up in the sky! Luckily, she remembered her parachute!

BROOKLYN BANKS

Beneath Brooklyn Bridge in New York City, USA, a wonderland of red-brick slopes, pillars and stairs nurtured street skaters like the Gonz from the 1980s. The Banks closed in 2010 but reopened in 2023 after campaigns from the skate community, bringing an iconic skatespot to a new generation of plywood pushers.

SAMARRIA THE BRAVE

Samarria Brevard learnt to kickflip by watching a Tony Hawk DVD borrowed from a library. Today, she is a street shredder, a powerful skater who tackles big stairs and big rails. Samarria has her own signature shoe with a dragonfly design, a symbol she chose for its colourfulness.

TALENTED TYSHAWN

Only three people have been *Thrasher* magazine's Skater of the Year twice, and Tyshawn Jones is one of them. This supremely talented New Yorker skates the odd comp, but he'd rather spend his time riding random obstacles on the street. Rubbish bins, benches and fountains – look out! Here comes Tyshawn!

VERT MASTERS

For some skaters, the only way is up – and up! Ramp riders with nerves of steel soar above giant half-pipes, spinning body and board in mind-boggling acrobatics. Let's fly high with two all-time aerial legends.

TONY 'THE BIRDMAN' HAWK

Tony was nine when his brother gave him a blue banana board – a present that changed his life.

He turned pro at 14 and has blazed an incredible trail ever since, winning 73 out of 103 pro contests, becoming *Thrasher*'s first-ever Skater of the Year and launching his own skateboard company and video games. His skill has earned him megabucks, but he also gives back by raising millions to build skateparks all over the world.

'The Birdman' has invented about 100 tricks, including the stalefish, frontside hurricane and rodeo flip.

Tony's first skateboard, the banana board, is on display at the National Museum of American History in Washington DC, USA.

A 12-time world champion, Tony has 16 X Games medals.

Tony landed the first-ever 900 (2.5 spins) in competition, at the 1999 X Games. His last 900 was in 2016, aged 48!

CARA-BETH BURNSIDE

Although Cara-Beth ('CB') skated alongside Tony Hawk, his megastardom was hard to reach. Skateboarding magazines in the 2000s were reluctant to feature women, and the prize money in competitions was always less. When Cara-Beth arrived at the 2005 X Games, the men's Vert first prize was $50,000; the women's just $2,000. Cara-Beth had had enough. She refused to leave her hotel room to compete until things changed. Her protest helped – the next year, first prize was increased to $15,000. And it was Cara-Beth who took Vert gold!

Cara-Beth became a pro snowboarder because it was hard to earn a living as a female skateboarder.

She has five X Games medals for skateboarding and three for snowboarding!

From the early 1980s to the mid-2000s (more than 30 years!), 'CB' was widely considered the best female vert skater in the world.

When 13-year-old Australian whizz kid Arisa Trew took Vert and Park golds at the 2023 X Games, she won the same prize money as the men's champions, thanks to Cara-Beth's campaigns.

OVER THE WALL!

The first time US pro Danny Way tried to skateboard over the Great Wall of China, in 2005, he fell and hurt his ankle. The next day, speeding at 80km/h down the five-storey-tall megaramp, he nailed a 360 air, sailing 19m over the wall!

POWER OF THE PEOPLE

Don't underestimate it. Passionate skaters all over the world are stirring things up – fighting for rights, skate-ifying cities and bringing skateboarding to disadvantaged kids. And then there are the skaters who made history by saving an iconic London skatespot . . .

LONG LIVE SOUTHBANK

If you walk along the River Thames in central London and peer into the shady forest of pillars beneath the Southbank Centre, you'll see skaters carving up an urban wonderland of criss-crossing ramps and concrete. It's been the heart of British skateboarding for more than 50 years and it's probably the oldest continually skated spot in the world. But in March 2013, a building project threatened to destroy it. There were plans to build a new skatepark nearby, but as the skaters who set up the Long Live Southbank (LLSB) group argued, "You can't move history!"

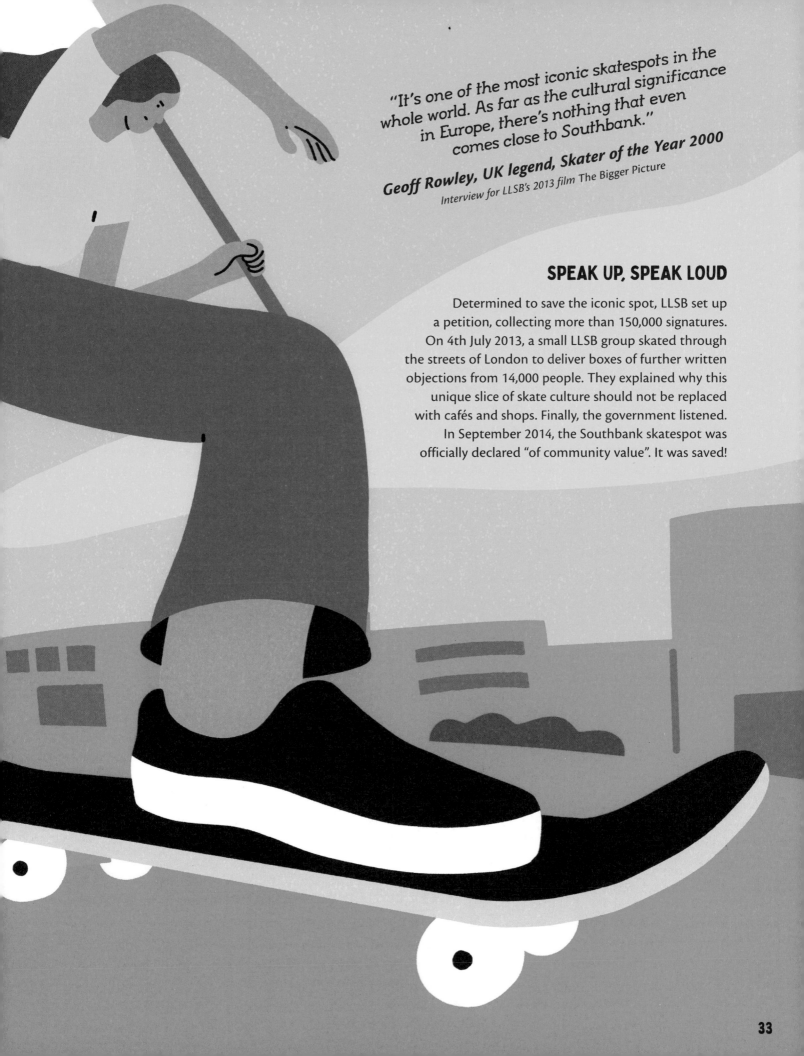

"It's one of the most iconic skatespots in the whole world. As far as the cultural significance in Europe, there's nothing that even comes close to Southbank."

Geoff Rowley, UK legend, Skater of the Year 2000
Interview for LLSB's 2013 film The Bigger Picture

SPEAK UP, SPEAK LOUD

Determined to save the iconic spot, LLSB set up a petition, collecting more than 150,000 signatures. On 4th July 2013, a small LLSB group skated through the streets of London to deliver boxes of further written objections from 14,000 people. They explained why this unique slice of skate culture should not be replaced with cafés and shops. Finally, the government listened. In September 2014, the Southbank skatespot was officially declared "of community value". It was saved!

FIGHT FOR YOUR RIGHTS

It's not always easy to jump on board. Some skateboarders have to deal with disabilities, skating bans or prejudice (unfair dislike). Let's drop in with three top skaters who never gave up fighting for their rights.

WHAT CAN YOU DO?

Want to save a skatepark or speak out about inequality or an unfair rule? Here's how to get your voice heard:

- Plan your argument. What needs to change? Why?
- Put yourself in other people's shoes. How does everyone feel?
- Get support. Could friends help? Would a teacher let you put up posters or start a school discussion?
- Can you email a local councillor or start an online petition?

BE YOURSELF, LEO BAKER

In 2020, talented pro Leo Baker had skated all the way to the USA's Olympic team. Leo is trans – a transgender person's gender identity is different to the one they were assigned at birth. Being trans in sport is tough, often because of people's prejudice. Leo really wanted to be himself and it didn't feel right competing in the women's team. So he had to quit. But Leo keeps flying the flag for the community by standing up for his rights and setting up a company supporting LGBTQ+ skaters.

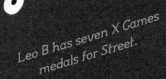

Leo B has seven X Games medals for Street.

BE THE CHANGE, LEO VALLS

Leo Valls was fed up with not being allowed to skate in parts of his hometown, Bordeaux, France. And he was fed up with skating fines and skatestoppers (notches on ledges and bumps on slopes that deter skaters). He began a campaign to show skateboarding as a positive force, not something to be feared or banned. Leo spoke to politicians, explaining why skateboarders skate streets, not just skateparks. He worked out how everyone could share public spaces respectfully. Today, Bordeaux is a super skate-friendly city. Bye-bye, skatestoppers. Hello, skateable sculptures!

Leo V loves making skate videos with his friends.

KEEP PUSHING, DAN MANCINA

At 13, Dan 'The Man' Mancina began losing his eyesight. It was hard, and for a while he gave up skateboarding. But then Dan realized he could still skate – just differently. Using a cane to feel for obstacles and listening for sound clues, he slowly built confidence. Today, Dan is a pro skater with a world record for a massive 6.9m 50–50 grind. He also runs skate workshops for visually impaired kids and is planning an adaptive skatepark for wheelchair users as well as skateboarders with limited vision.

Dan's signature board has braille on the underside. A cut-out notch helps him find the nose.

CHANGE THE WORLD

People power is spreading the joy of skating all over the world. By building skateparks for disadvantaged kids or providing kit to those who can't afford it, skaters are pulling together to create safe spaces to meet up, make friends and share their love for going wild on wheels.

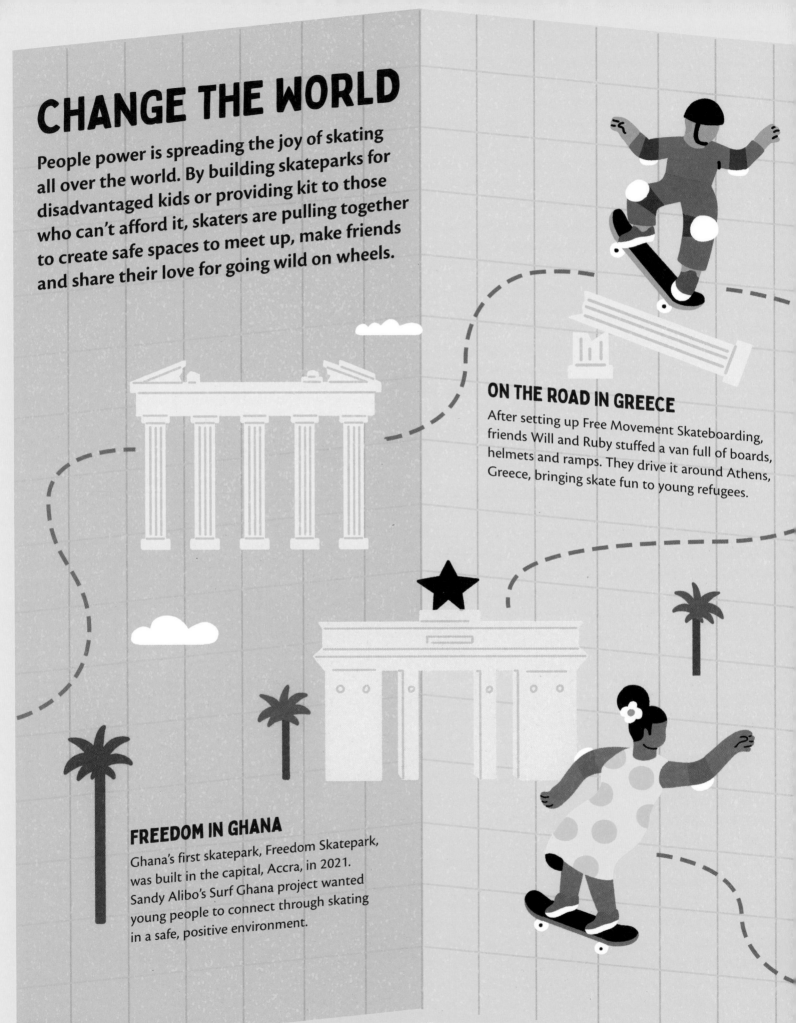

ON THE ROAD IN GREECE

After setting up Free Movement Skateboarding, friends Will and Ruby stuffed a van full of boards, helmets and ramps. They drive it around Athens, Greece, bringing skate fun to young refugees.

FREEDOM IN GHANA

Ghana's first skatepark, Freedom Skatepark, was built in the capital, Accra, in 2021. Sandy Alibo's Surf Ghana project wanted young people to connect through skating in a safe, positive environment.

WHAT CAN YOU DO?

Want to do your bit to help less fortunate kids around the world? You could:

- Look up the groups on these pages with an adult. How can you help them?
- Raise money for a cause you believe in – perhaps with a cake sale or a sponsored skate?
- Find out if there's a place near you where you can donate old boards, pads and helmets.

CARIBBEAN SKATEPARK

In San Luis, Dominican Republic, San Skate offers free lessons at its skatepark to help disadvantaged kids have a break from – and see a different life beyond – the tough conditions on the streets.

CAMBODIA ON WHEELS

The Skateistan site in Phnom Penh, Cambodia, has a 500m² skatepark, a library and a classroom. Local children, some with disabilities, come to learn as well as to skate. A few even return as instructors when they're older!

GIRL SKATE INDIA

In 2016, Indian pro Atita Verghese toured her home country with her crew, Girl Skate India, building a DIY ramp and teaching young girls to skateboard. In 2018, US pro Lizzie Armanto dropped in on Atita in Bangalore to help run a workshop.

"My style of skateboarding is vert. I love flying and that feeling of the wind . . . I love flying and that feeling of the wind . . . It feels like it's lifting you up to another dimension."

Gui Khury, Brazilian vert prodigy
2021 Interview for Whistle's No Days Off video series

THE X GAMES

Back in the early 90s in the US, TV viewers were getting bored watching football and baseball. The first 'Extreme Games' in 1995 was a game-changer, showcasing bungee jumping, roller-blading and climbing. Today, Summer, Winter and Asian X Games beam BMX, motocross and snowboarding all over the world. Skateboarding has been part of the crew since the beginning, with gnarly Park and Street events, and aerial madness in Vert, Big Air and MegaPark. Over the years, X Games prize pots and TV coverage has sprinkled a little extra fame and fortune onto skateboarders such as Street gold medalists Shane O'Neill from Australia and Momiji Nishiya from Japan.

MEGARAMP MEGASTAR

It's a long way down. But Gui Khury can handle an 8m-high X Games megaramp. This young Brazilian has competed at the Games since he was ten – the youngest ever competitor. At 11, he was the first to land a 1080 on a vert ramp; at 12, he was the youngest to win X Games gold (Vert Best Trick, 2021). At the 2023 X Games, 14-year-old Gui was the youngest of all the MegaPark competitors. The event was held at 'Sloanyard' – vert legend Elliot Sloan's personal megaramp in California. Over fives runs, Gui soared over the gap onto the huge quarter-pipe, knocking out 900s and other aerial wizardry to bag silver. He also won Vert Best Trick gold for a jaw-dropping 900 judo. His secret? Practising spins on a trampoline!

LET THE GAMES BEGIN

Do you think skateboarding is a sport? Are skaters athletes? Well, competitions have been around since the 1960s, when skateboarders wowed judges with handstands and wheelies. Today, pro skaters bust out their best moves at Dew Tour, Street League (SLS), the World Championships and, from 2021, the Olympics. But it was at the X Games where competitions really took off

ROAD TO THE OLYMPICS

Fancy going for gold? It's a long way to that podium, and any pro will tell you the Olympic journey is full of twists and turns, bumps, failures and falls. But let's give it a go and see if we can ride all the way to gold!

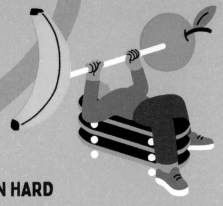

2. TRAIN HARD

Your coach may set you a training schedule, with several sessions a week alongside school, plus some strength-training in the gym. Remember to eat well and sleep well.

1. MAKE THE TEAM

Search online for your national skateboarding organization and find out how to make their team. Good comp results, dedication and a video showing solid skills will impress them.

Don't crash into the camera operator – like Australian Kieran Woolley did during his Tokyo Olympic Park run. Oof!

Felipe Nunes has gone 360 on Tony Hawk's infamous Loop!

Yuto Horigome won Street gold in his Tokyo, Japan, hometown at the 2020 Olympics Games (held in 2021).

FLIP IT, FELIPE!

Let's hope skateboarding becomes a Paralympic sport because athletes like Brazilian Felipe Nunes, who lost both his legs aged six, have supersick skills. He has podiumed at the X Games and won both Park and Street at Dew Tour.

3. RANK SKY-HIGH

Only 88 skateboarders make it to the Olympics – 22 men and 22 women for both Park and Street. (Sorry, ramp riders, there's no Vert just yet.) To be an Olympian, aim high in World Skate's rankings. Rack up ranking points at comps in the two years before the Games – the World Championships counts, but X Games doesn't.

When GB athlete Sky Brown became Park world champion in 2023, she topped the rankings with 80,000 points.

4. HIT THE OLYMPIC PARK

Welcome to the Olympics! Get to know the skatepark with a few practice sessions. The first-ever Olympic skatepark, built for Tokyo 2020, had a huge street plaza packed with rails and ramps, steps and banks, plus a massive park bowl up to 3.5m deep with a central volcano.

5. IMPRESS THE JUDGES

Time for the prelims! Wow the judges with 45-second runs (plus five of your best tricks for Street). Balance difficulty with style and flow, and try to make use of the whole course. Aim for big airs and clean landings. Usually only the top eight make it to the finals – so bring on your best moves!

6. GO FOR GOLD

You did it! You're in the finals! Now, if you want to make it to the top of the podium, you'll need to nail those runs and land your trickiest tricks. Go for it, champ!

KEEP ON ROLLING

It's been a wild ride – from swimming pools to Olympic bowls, flatground farmyards to massive megaramps. We've skated across the world and we've been inspired by battles for equality. But what's next? What do you think skateboarding's future holds? How much faster and higher should it ride? How far from its original roots should it roll?

> **"I KEEP SKATING BECAUSE IT'S ALWAYS BROUGHT ME THE MOST JOY AND IT CONTINUES TO EVOLVE . . . I STILL CAN DO IT, SO WHY WOULD I EVER QUIT?"**
>
> *Tony Hawk*
> **2022 short film for Vanity Fair magazine**

Some want skateboarding to stay close to its origins – think rule-free rebel riders, not big business sports and online stars. But hopefully, as skateboarding grows, changes and eats up mainstream culture, there will be space for all.

We need that space for more skateparks for learners, more training facilities for athletes and more shared urban spots for street riders. There are already cafés with ramped walls and shopping centres with bowls, but how do we create more spaces like this? Understanding skateboarding better will help. Understanding its long, rich history and its friendly culture of easy acceptance – differences don't matter when your feet are planted on plywood. A love for skateboarding unites all kinds of people.

Views are already changing. The Olympics helped people to see skateboarding as a sport, and everyone knows that sports and exercise are good for the body and mind. We're talking strong legs and a healthy heart, we're talking exercising outdoors, away from screens and with real-life human beings! And, most of all, we're talking about the way skateboarding can free us from our worries. How when we skate we can think of nothing else, only the movement, only the fun.

So tell your friends about the pool-riders of the 1970s, tell your parent or guardian about the international skate projects and tell your teacher that they have skateboarders to thank for their favourite pair of trainers.

But don't just talk – go skating! Keep pushing and keep positive. And however you roll . . .

SKATE SAFE
SKATE FUN
SKATE YOU

PIGEON CREW

GLOSSARY

50-50 GRIND
A grind with both trucks centred over the rail or edge.

360
One full rotation (360 degrees) of body and board.

900
Two and a half rotations of body and board.

AIR
An aerial trick, often above lip of bowl or ramp.

BANANA BOARD
A small, narrow skateboard.

BANK
A flat, skateable slope.

BEARINGS
Round metal pieces inside wheels that attach to the trucks.

BIG AIR
A former X Games vert event on a megaramp.

BLOCK
A small, skateable obstacle, sometimes with reinforced edges.

BOARDSLIDE
Sliding on the deck along an edge.

BOWL
A swimming-pool shaped structure with curved sides, a flat bottom and coping on the lip.

COPING
The metal edging on the lip of ramps, pipes and bowls for slides and grinds.

DROP IN
Balancing the tail of a board on coping and leaning forwards to skate into a bowl, ramp or pipe.

FISHTAIL
An often wide board with a back end shaped into two points like a fish's tail.

FLATGROUND
A flat, featureless, skateable surface, rather than a vert or obstacled area.

FLOW PARK
A skatepark combining street and transition features that can be skated in continuous flowing lines.

FREESTYLE
A style of skateboarding in which tricks are performed on flatground without using transitions or street features.

FRONTSIDE
When a skater's body is facing the direction of travel or an obstacle. ('Backside' is when their back faces the direction of travel or an obstacle.)

FRONTSIDE HURRICANE
A grind trick – a 180 (half rotation of skater and board) onto a rail, landing on the back truck.

GRIND
Sliding on the trucks along an edge.

GRIPTAPE
The sandpaper-like layer stuck to the top of the deck to give riders more grip.

HALF-PIPE
Two quarter-pipes joined with a flat section.

JUDO
Grabbing the heel edge of the front of the board while kicking the front foot forwards.

KICKFLIP
Spinning the board mid-ollie by using the front foot to flip the board's heel edge.

MEGAPARK
An X Games vert event on a megaramp.

MEGARAMP
A specialized ramp for pro comps – a tall launch ramp, then a large gap onto a high quarter-pipe.

OLLIE
Jumping with the board by pushing the back foot onto the tail and leaping as the front pops up.

PARK
A style of skateboarding – transition and vert skating in a skatepark bowl.

PLYWOOD
A material made from several thin layers of wood glued together. Decks are usually made from seven layers of Canadian maple wood.

POPSICLE
A classic skateboard shape. The nose and tail are equally rounded (like a lollipop stick) and tilt up at the same angle.

PRO
Short for 'professional' or 'professional person' – someone who is paid for their work or skills.

PYRAMID
A flat-topped, pyramid-shaped skateable obstacle.

QUARTER-PIPE
A single curved ramp.

RAIL
A metal railing or stairway handrail for grinds and slides.

RODEO FLIP
A 540 frontside spin (one and a half rotations) in which the skater goes upside down at the same time. Invented by Tony Hawk in 1984.

SIDEWALK
US word for 'pavement'. 'Sidewalk surfer' is a nickname for a skateboarder.

SLAM
A hard fall.

SLASH GRIND
Grinding on the back truck while turning on a ramp's coping.

STALEFISH
A grab trick – using your back hand to grab the heel edge of the board in between the feet.

STREET
A style of skateboarding – riding urban features such as benches and rails on the streets or in a skatepark.

STREET PLAZA
A skatepark area with obstacles for street skating.

SWITCH-STANCE
When a 'regular' rider (left foot forwards) rides 'goofy' (right foot forwards) – or vice-versa.

TRANSITION
A bank or curved ramp.

VERT
A style of skateboarding – riding transitions and vert ramps.

VERT RAMP
A large (3 to 5m high) half-pipe with a flat bottom transitioning to vertical sides.

VOLCANO
A cone-shaped skateable obstacle with a flat top.